POSSIBILITY

A MEMOIR ON FALLING
IN LOVE
IN HATE
IN SORROW

A.G.LEDESMA

For the youth of the world who feel alone.

Tomorrow will be better.

And if not,

Say it until it becomes the truth.

You will one day find yourself looking down at the mountain of pain you trekked.

Until then, I'm rooting for you.

For my Grandma Carolyn.

For that young girl I was, who hadn't known the dread she felt was anxiety and what was to come.

It gets better.

POSSIBILITY

I get that I just might not be the right fit for you
and that all of this mess of poetry is useless,
but I have held on for so long
that I have become used to the pain
and agony of unrequited love.

 My awareness of loving you is scorched on my heart,
where you have branded me
with the words "Possibility."
And because of that my life has taken
a complete turn into a black zone.
A barren void where I convince myself
that this is the best that it's going to get.

So sometimes people get caught in the wrong place
at the wrong time,
or we fall in love with the wrong person,
at an erroneous age
and sometimes It snows in April.

I guess to preface this, when I was six years old, I met Lisa Campbell Ernst, the author of *'Goldilocks Returns'* in my little elementary school in the smelly cow-plant town of Garden City, Kansas. I think that encounter set the course of the next decade of my life because it was then I realized people could just make stories and put them out into the world to be read. I was an early reader; I didn't realize until recently just how strange it was that I was six and finishing up the *'Junie B. Jones'* series by myself. I had already loved reading but meeting that author just presented the idea that would never come to leave my mind, that I would want to write something of my own to share with the world.

It was a silent dream for the majority of my childhood. My family had grown to know I enjoyed reading but I had never shared my thoughts on wanting to write, especially since I had no clue exactly what I wanted to write. I remember learning about poetry at school in the fifth grade, and again the course of my life altered to fit this new information. I wrote my first poem at ten years old and my teacher at the time was at a loss of what to say about my piece. Other children had written rhyming poems about nature or some based off video games or cartoons but mine was titled *'POSSIBILITY'* and I had wrote about a boy I had *"loved"* (or as much as a ten year old could possibly love for that age) I used a thesaurus for the bigger words of the piece to fully convey how much it hurt to have such unacknow-ledged feelings. I didn't tell anyone about the praise I got that day, I kept it to myself. I had the piece written in a notebook and I just couldn't shake the feeling that I was doing something big.

I wrote other pieces over the years, just putting them away in a folder. It wasn't until middle school that I started saving them into a document on a computer. Since most of the poems I had written around that time pertained to that unrequited love of my youth, this work was originally titled *"The Unrequited Love"*, very edgy and very cheesy. From there, seeing the work compiled into one I realized I was really typing up the first rough draft of a book. And not just any book, a poetry book. Along the way this book was constantly evolving through the many phases and milestones of my adolescence. The meaning changed constantly, and my muses came and went.

At some point I started struggling with my mental health severely. As a teenager I became clinically depressed and suicidal to the point that this book became one big goodbye letter to my loved ones. It became an incessant cycle of hating myself, hating the situation and hating my family. It was just two years of unexplainable hatred and sadness and hormones all wrapped up in angsty poems. I don't mean to disregard those feelings because it was all very real and very scary and to this day, I'm still struggling with the aftereffects of it all and still nursing my chronic depression. I can surely say that this book is no longer a goodbye.

And then I turned eighteen. I had reached an age I never thought possible, and I struggled with the concept of still being alive. If this sounds silly, then good for you. If this sounds familiar, I'm sorry. I blacked out pretty much most of 18-20. Most of those years were spent trying to write, feeling numb and liking BTS. I was supposed to publish this whole work in 2020 to close off the second decade of my life, but of course COVID became a thing that pretty much took my whole entire life off course and I had lost any passion I had for writing, and I was pretty much ready to delete this whole project and forget about this whole dream. I thought because it wasn't going to happen in 2020 that it was never going to happen. I dropped out of college. I threw myself into work and helped take care of my little sisters and just ignored this giant file of written feelings.

Well thanks to the grace of my grandma Carolyn, I'm finishing this thing once and for all. I've spent the majority of 2022 trying to rekindle my love for writing. I rejoined old fanfiction sites I used to write for and day by day I've written little pieces here and there and now I'm tackling this beast.

This work is titled POSSIBILITY for many different reasons, in dedication to my first piece, in dedication to the unrequited love that sparked this whole madness, in reference to my mental health and now in reference to the outcome of me finally achieving my dreams. Cause' there's a possibility this will become everything I hoped it would be and more.

This book is a memoir from my adolescence. From the first feelings of love to the unavoidable angst and hate that comes with growing up and the sorrow that sneaks in when you least expect it. I'm finishing this book to prove to myself and my family that this isn't goodbye. That I'm here for the long run and I'm going to achieve my dreams while I'm at it.

Thank you, friends and family, for your patience, thank you for believing in this possibility.

22

(p.s. I was born in the year 2000, meaning when I put a number at the end of a piece, it's for both the year and my age.) :)

IN LOVE

BRIMSTONE

I am stained a terrible green color.

I am strained to never love another.

    It is for you, my heart sprints at one hundred miles a minute.

It is for you, my head is constantly reeling with my feelings for you and all the things that you do,

and the constant theme in most of these poems is that you have no clue how much I absolutely adore you.

    You have provided me with two second glances,
    and a smile you'd give to a stranger on a public bus

For this is how my love story goes

it is a girl with a journal over-analyzing every moment shared with him and copying it all down just so she can send it out on the internet to be eaten up by fellow humans who believe that they feel her pain.

But they couldn't possibly know what it feels like to be stained with green.

12

MY COWARDICE

Unrequited love is falling in love,
with no lover to catch you.

I have often told myself,
"If we were meant to be together we will."

But most times I am not that strong to believe
the words that have tumbled past my lips
in a moment of reassurance.

This game that I am trapped in
is no longer fun,
it seems never ending,

    But my damn heart,
it insists on seeing what is the prize
for finishing this game,

Is it to win him?
 or myself?

13

INSOMNIA

When I attempt to close my eyes for the night,
My heart picks up a pen and holds it tight.
I toss and turn between wrong and right.
I think about how much longer
I can continue to fight.

Insomnia such a sweet sounding word,
the way it rolls off your tongue
and onto the splintered floorboards.

I suffer when I'm awake
with sight of you,
and I am taunted when I am asleep
with dreams of you.

Insomnia is the purgatory
between living and dreaming,
and you're still there.

You're everywhere.

MEDIOCRE

My heart
will always be heavy
with my love for you.

16

HADES

Baptized by the belief
that I will gain eternal happiness
 if I follow ten simple rules.

My life is a living hell,

Because I am without you.

16

THE 7TH

When I told you to your face
that I didn't believe in love,
and you actually believed me.

Lies have always come easily to me,
get me into more trouble than they don't.

But to be sitting across from you,
saying, "I don't believe in love
because I have no true foundation that it exists."

Screw foundation,
screw security,
I don't need that
when I have you.

13

HIGHLIGHT

No one told me I was going to find you.

There wasn't a warning,

Or Prophecy set out.

It was just a matter of being in the right place

At the right time.

It was a matter of a ten year old,

Who made the decision to let you rest in her heart.

And it's a matter of a seventeen year old,

Who decided to never let you go.

17

I SHOULD'VE SAID SOMETHING

You know what's worse
than having a nightmare about you?

It's having a good dream about you.

Because no matter how much
I want it to come true, it never will.

You're my impossible thought.

I dreamt I was back in that town.
Where you whispered
how much you loved me.

You want to know what's worse
than having a good dream about you?

Not dreaming about you at all.

15

MODERN ROMANCE

Out of all the people
I could've made a connection with
in this world
Of course, it just had to be the one
who was furthest from my reach.

15

ANGUISH

People worry about things
They cannot control.

I worry about death.
I worry about my heart.
I worry about you.

I am rich with worry.

12

KIDDIE STUFF

You sat with her at lunch today.
Your leg was bouncing like crazy,
and your face was all red.

Did you know you make me feel that way?

15

NEROSIS

I am a broken record.
I repeat the same sayings,
Cry about the same issues,
and I love you.
To be unable to define yourself
without the one you call soulmate
is almost as if someone was carrying a vase
only to shatter it to pieces.
And no matter how hard you try to put it back together,
there's always going to be slivers of shards
missing among the cracks in the wood.
And this is the troubling thing,
I know deep down in my heart,
that I belong to him.
But he is not mine.
He is not mine to think of,
to dream,,
to hold,
to love.

He is not mine to love.

MUTE

If I get any closer,
you're going to drain
the life out of me.

You've already taken my words.
And my love.
Take it all.

17

ADONIS BLUE

To see you again,
After three months of going without
my daily dosage of your eyes,
I can now once again
claim you as my unhealthy obsession.

But my heart still aches in pain
at the thought of you having no knowledge of my love.
I always thought I was an obvious creature,
My feelings written upon my sleeve.

But I guess the dense are blind to what is written.

13

APHRODITE

What kind of monster would I be,

If I told you I loved you,

When you're in love with someone else?

17

ATTACUS ATLAS

I've prayed for you often.
Almost every night,
I hoped for your wellbeing.

In the same breath I prayed to have you.
Devoid of respect,
it's sinful to covet.

But if being locked out of heaven
meant that I'd have you in my arms,
sign me the fuck up.

16

VICEROY

How does it feel to know that you pushed away the girl who worshiped your imperfections?

I mean, I have no clue as to whether or not you're going to read this, but if you are...

Do you know that this is about you?

Within my words do you understand that these words are for you?

Compiled into a form of poetry this is an open love letter to you.

And everyone else who were unable to return the love I have given them, but you.

You are the final goodbye.

After I have torn everyone else to shreds,

you are the last one standing.

Because you couldn't possibly know that this is for you, could you?

DROUGHT

I misplaced the love
I was supposed to give myself.
Living day in and day out,
For six whole years
in an abysmal black void.

Only to see that I had given it all to you.
Every sickly sweet drop,
But you weren't parched to begin with.

16

1732

Who would've thought
that in this day of age,
someone from such a great distance
got a hold of such a great piece of my heart.

Because you,
and only you
Shall receive
the best parts of me.

Even if you decide
you don't want them.
They're all useless
without you.

17

PIERIDAE

Why have we come to fear love?

I have come all this way, on an epic journey of discovery.
Readying myself to tell you that I have loved you
for the past seven years with every piece of my very being.
I granted you ownership of my heart
before I even realized you don't want it.

I fear breaking both of our hearts in the process.

I fear that my efforts have gone to waste,
because although you deserve my love and much more...
I cannot begin to count the missed opportunities
I've been given to replace the love I have given you,
to give to myself.

Because I still have yet to write myself a love poem.

17

LUNA

With each *"I love you"* you've tacked onto
the end of your messages,
this feeling became more real.

I am falling for a person I can't even touch.

17

RHOPALOCERA

What are the odds
that we're in love
with the same person?

What are the odds
That I love her more
Than you ever could?

17

PATAKI

Don't underestimate the will of a girl in love.
Don't waste your time trying to offer her affection.
Don't waste your time trying to go to war with her.

She doesn't want you.
It's a harsh fact to swallow.
I know.

But for your own good,
Don't waste your time
On a girl who's already wasted
on someone else.

15

MY BEAN

"Thank u for dealing w my UGLIE pics and annyoing rants,,
i love u so much and idk what i would do w/o you.
You've helped me through rough times
and i cant thank u enough."
"ALSO THANK YOU FOR THE DANK MEMES."
-Hanna Pomeroy

16

(You sent this to me at 2 am after you opened up to me about some crazy stuff happening in your life. You once told me that those aren't things, you'd talk about with anyone, and yet you chose me. Just a weird girl who lives 1732 miles away. You trust me and that means the world to me. I trust you as well. You are my best friend, no matter the distance, no matter the time zones, you're my other half and I love you more than you'll ever know.)

PREACHER MAN

Sold my heart to the Devil.
Turned my back on God.

I fell in love without it,
Stuck in between`
Something unrequited
And something that can't be seen.

You could say that I have adapted,
Or you could say
that with each breath I take
Is another step closer
Out of this personal hell
I built for us.

I NEEDED THIS TO GO WRONG

YOU HAVE CRASHED INTO MY LIFE
LIKE A SHOOTING STAR,
I WAS BLINDED BY A LIGHT
THAT ONCE SEEMED SO FAR
NOW THE LIGHT IS GONE,
AND MY EYES HAVEN'T ADJUSTED
TO THIS DARKNESS
YOU'VE RUINED ME.

15

NEW ERA

after six years, you will never ever get a clue
of how deep my feelings were for you
but it's time to let go
for this has to end

I want something new
I want something that's not you

12

BIRDWING

I never got the chance to say goodbye.
In the darkness the color isn't just black.

>   *It is bright green.*

A color i wish I had never seen

How can this be fair to me?
To lay awake at night
Wishing for you.

>   *Wishing for you*
>   *to wish for me too.*

11

PROBLEMS EVOLVE TO LOVE

Everything stemmed from loving a boy who will never love me back, to loving a girl who I can never have, to loving myself for it's what has been missing this whole time.

Because you're always told how simple it is to fall in love.

Like breathing.

You're always told to love unconditionally, to be kind, to cherish.

But you're never told how to not fall in love.

And I was never taught how to love myself.

I try to manage through every day to see myself in a better light.

But I still can't help but think

I'm not what you wanted.

18

TWILIGHT

And onc day out of nowhere,
You became the voice
Of my conscience.

You told me right from wrong,
You made witty jokes,
You fueled a mess of poetry.

And I think that's why
I can't let you go.
Because somehow, someway
You becoming the voice in my head
You have unintentionally
became a part of me.

And I'd rather be taunted by you
Then not hearing you at all.

13

COUP DE FOUDRE

How could you not know that I love you?

Isn't my heart screaming loud enough?

18

PERSEID

I can't keep thinking things are coincidences,
because when it's 3 in the morning for me
and midnight for you
and I'm crying
and how much I wish to message you about it right now
but I can't because you have school.
But you message me in that exact instant
to tell me about how much you love me.
This is no coincidence

It was my heart reaching for you
And it was yours reaching for me too.

18

WOULDN'T IT BE NICE

I really put you on a pedestal, didn't I?

I would wake up in the morning thinking about you, about your dreams and if you saw what I saw. I would go through my day imagining that you were right there beside me and this person I made you out to be was actually the one I fell in love with.

You both just seem to have the same face.

I dreamt up the perfect person for me in your image rendering me completely useless to this charm I thought you possessed, and now that I'm not a prepubescent little girl, I can see it all very clearly. I was under a goddamn spell for eight fucking years and now at eighteen I see you in the hallway and I wait for my heart to fall in the pit of my stomach and when it doesn't I'm so fucking confused that I make eye contact with you for the first time in 3 months.

It has been one hell of a depressing summer. so much so that I didn't even have the brain capacity to think about you.
Now of course there's still things I can't help.

You're absolutely gorgeous. And I would literally take a bullet for you. I value that you represent my first love and that you unknowingly helped get me through a tough time in my life.

You see, the year I met you was the same year my parents were having problems. And when I fell in love with you my mother had left. And it sucks to rip the veil off of all of this but I used my love for you to get away from my problems at home.

And this just makes every poem and love letter quite depressing, and just know to not underestimate the talents of a ten year old girl and the legacy she built because she saw how easily things could fall apart.

18

FINSTA

I fall in love with people who are unattainable,

I isolate myself out of fear of ruining the friendships I barely have, ruining them even more.

I distrust anyone who gets close because I feel that there's always someone better and that every special moment i've ever had with them meant nothing to them.

I don't fight to keep people in my life because if I mattered enough they would stay. all the people that didn't stay took a piece of me with them and I honestly feel like if I lose anyone else I'm going to fucking lose my mind.

18

GODS AND NEIGHBORS

So far, I don't regret a single person
I've bared my soul to.

And that in itself is a win.
A huge win.

15

I'VE GOTTA LOTTA LOVIN' TO DO

It's strange, but I tried my very hardest to find warmth within the coldest hearts.

I fell in love with two someones I could never have.

And that has scarred me and turned me away from the concept of love completely because I was being a big baby about it. I thought that I was unlovable just because I couldn't have them. I went into a spiral of self hate and insecurities just from two shitty experiences. And I fall in love for the dumbest and over-thought moments. I fell in love with him because he was nice to me when I felt like my world was falling apart. And I fell in love with her because she was showing me the purest form of love I had ever experienced. Although I have yet to experience a romantic, requited love, it doesn't make the other two less real. I've felt love in every aspect with both of them because I have a lot of love to give.

Just because it wasn't what I wanted it to be doesn't mean they didn't matter.

Just know my heart is dissected into many pieces but it doesn't mean I love you less.

18

MOONSTRUCK

This back and forth of lovey feelings
and my depression is giving me whiplash
Because it seems as if when I'm not in love,
I'm depressed and if I'm not depressed, I'm in love.

18

(Don't tie the value of yourself to another human being.)

[REDACTED]

You being in my life has changed things around so drastically.

Before you I'd never thought of the future on such a big scale with such big dreams, I had one wish and it was to leave home, but you showed me that instead of running away from these things I should be running towards better things.

You've pushed me to seeing the potential I have,

you showed me how truly competitive I am

and I felt like I could confide my darkest truths to you.

In the back of my mind, I've always known I loved you. But for once in my life, I just wanted a friend that I knew I didn't have to be afraid of losing them.

18

SEPTEMBER: THE MONTH FOR FALLING

You loved me wrong.

18

(something that was hard to say and to write)

RATIOCINATE

Tied my hands behind my back.
Blindfolded my heart
So I couldn't fall in love this time.

Because with you it would've been so easy.

And that's what I think hurts the most.
I'm not letting myself indulge in a fantasy anymore.
Because if I'm being honest,
I don't think I deserve to be happy with you,

You're too pure
Too good.

And I'd only ruin that.

18

BOY BLUE

A Seattle crewneck
Your speckled peach fuzz face.
Anytime you leaned in to whisper in my ear
I held myself back with a strength I didn't know I had.
I let moments slip through my fingers
because I am already yours.

18

(you didn't deserve this, but I wrote it anyway.)

EVENFALL

I am so in love with you
and so sure of you in this moment
that I don't even have to hesitate thinking
about the next moment.

18

(how could I be mad at you
when you helped me write love poems again?)

ORANGE

I keep telling myself to get rid of high expectations, that when you're expecting nothing to happen something does happen, but I want to expect that he likes me as much as I like him.

I want to have this expectation that I'm making the right fucking move and that this isn't all for nothing.

18

OVER AGAIN

I haven't been able to get you outta my head.

And I keep trying to look up on google if it's a scientific fact that when you think of someone, it's because they're thinking of you too.

But I won't hold my breath.

It's always like this for me, I have obsessive habits born from being a One Direction fan and being so afraid of the one I like or even love moving on without knowledge of my feelings. I've only gotten passed the confession threshold twice and both times it was so horrific to the point where I never braved it out to cross again so instead, I take the smallest chances, send the smallest hints, read too far into every gesture because of how fucking desperate I have come to be, just for someone to dote on, to love and to be loved back I hold no other honor.

I break my own heart
   and I'm pretty fucking good at it too.

18

THE VIRGIN

I'll write you cute love notes everyday if you want me to.
 I'll name a star after you.
Just say the word and I'll do whatever you ask of me

I'm yours, I'm yours, I'm yours.

Even if what you ask of me is to go.
I'll go. Just don't misuse my heart.
Don't take this love for granted.

I'm yours, I'm yours, I'm yours.

18

(This one was cheesy and dumb and to the beat of my heart
 I kept it around because this was the best part
about being in love,
thinking that it'd be like that forever.)

PRAXITELES

I'm just not the type of person people fall for.
And that's the troubling thing.

That someone who sculpts words of love
has no one to dote on.

15

THIS WASN'T SUPPOSED TO BE ABOUT YOU

Tired of being tired.
Tired of feelings that I shouldn't be feeling
for people I can't have.
Tired of being numb when those feelings
become too much.
This wasn't supposed to be about you,
but that's just how everything ends up these days.

When I don't see you I'm restless.
When I do, I feel okay again.

Tired of letting these feelings dictate my wellbeing.
Tired of falling for people that like me
but never love me.
And I got so much of it to give. What a waste.
This wasn't supposed to be about you, but it is.
It always is.

20

TOTSIENS

A setting sun and solitude.
Bags under my eyes and pearlescent moon.

I can't close my eyes
I don't want to see you anymore.

13

LACUNA

Is the moon still in love with the sun?

Does she still wait for him every day?

Do her craters still make her cry?

18

THE FIRST TIME WE HAD TO SAY GOODBYE

Seeing you for the first time
I didn't think about the after effects.
I didn't know at the time
what it felt like to actually miss you.
The first time I met you
was also the first time we ever had to say goodbye.
I told you all about Kansas bugs and sunsets,
But I forgot to tell you I love you.

18

THIS MUST BE THE PLACE

Would you ever come to know this lonely side of me?

One that forbids you to leave my mind

and yet too stubborn to ask you to stay?

16

INSIPIENCE

When I was with you,
it was like I finally got a break from the pain.
When I want something really bad,
I have a tendency to ruin things for myself.

I smothered myself in this feeling
and I suffocated thinking it was love
and I died knowing you wouldn't love me back.

This could've been something so simple yet so necessary.
Again, when I was given your hand I tried to take you whole.
I made myself believe you were all that I wanted.

I've made a nasty habit of falling for friends
and forgetting that romance means nothing
if not reciprocated.
It's the same incessant cycle,
I have yet to learn my lesson.

I have yet to triumph over this side of myself
That tells me I can't be happy if I'm alone.

19

DON'T LEAVE ME YOUNG

I should have hugged you harder the last time I saw you.
Please my love, don't leave me young.

What about the plans we had made?
In my life all I see is you.
In this life there's no me without you.

So please my love,
don't leave me young.

19

STEP 1 OF 1000

I won't be moved

You come back to me with tears in your eyes. I'm in shock because this is the first time I have seen you cry. You were getting ready to take a second chance. And our life flashed past my eyes.

I won't be moved

It was clear before me what would happen if I let you stay. You have this ability to pick up the pieces I'm lacking. You would spend months doing so. You would make me feel whole again. You would be in my head telling me everything I wanted to hear and in the same instance you would blame me. I blame myself.

I can't be moved.

I never thought that I could ever be strong enough to look you in the eyes and tell you no. It almost ripped me apart to do so. That deep guttural feeling of doing something to love yourself for the first time, it's bittersweet. It fucking hurt like hell and it was the first step out of a thousand to begin loving myself.

I want to move

HOW MANY TIMES CAN I FALL IN LOVE BEFORE THE DECADE'S OVER?

At one point I looked at you and decided I never wanted to look at anyone else.

19

(I never know when I'm past the point of no return.)

REGAINING BALANCE DURING AN EARTHQUAKE

Read this to show what you really have.

  -The mindless girl ready to die for you.

16

CRYING ON FACETIME

"Okay, bye I'm going to jump off of the earth."

"The earth isn't flat, silly."

"Times like these make me wish it was."

19

(When boys make your heart hurt.)

YOU ALWAYS HURT THE ONE YOU LOVE

We were doomed from the start.
Too young for broken hearts.

Trying to be strong when it makes no sense to hold on
You gotta let go,
you did all that you could, and they know

They were doomed from the start.
Couldn't fix the broken parts.

Some love is too strong to be kept.

16

TELL ME WHERE IT HURTS

The pain of learning I had you all along
and I didn't even know it.

The pain of revelation,
that you loved me the entire time I had loved you
and that still wasn't enough.

The pain of letting you go a second time.

The pain of knowing we were too late,
and it wasn't meant to be.

The pain of leaving.
Of saying goodbye.
Of never kissing you.
Of never fully explaining you were the love of my life.

The pain of never seeing you again.

22

(The pain of still loving you.)

MELPOMENE AND THALIA

I've been trying to fix this. I've been trying to hold my own hand and not imagine it being yours. I've been trying to wake up and take the next step towards feeling whole.

I honestly don't think I even know what that feels like.

A majority of my life I always remember having to read a room. How to understand which sighs mean fight and which ones mean flight. I have the tendency to let people walk all over me. It's only fitting I became a waitress.

Becoming aware of how much I'm catering to other people's feelings and suppressing my own has awoken me to the illusions I've set for myself. Coming to grasp the different alters I've built for my selves to mask and present. I've come to realize I'm the biggest imposter I'll ever come to know.

When you said you loved me, did you just mean the version of myself I thought you would want?

22

LOVE AND EPIPHANY

There's been a release of anguish I've been avoiding for five years.

There's a new wave of love and heartbreak for this boy I didn't know I could achieve.

Love, because I realized I never stopped loving him.

Heartbreak, because I realized I will never stop loving him.

Love, because so many parts of my confused younger self finally has the answers to her many questions. Due to his courage. Due to his love and epiphany.

Heartbreak, because if only those words had come sooner. Maybe we both wouldn't be nursing these wounded hearts.

I loved you with everything I had and I'm just now realizing the damage it may have caused to the both of us.

Heartbreak, because I don't know how to help him.

Heartbreak, because how could someone do this to you?

Heartbreak, because you can't love me without thinking about her.

Heartbreak, because I can't love you without thinking of you, thinking about her.

22

YOU TOLD ME YOU LOVED ME IN APRIL

Maybe this is how it was always supposed to be.

Maybe I will never get over you and you will move on and be the greatest version of yourself, only empowered at the thought of knowing you left me behind.

And maybe I deserve it.

22

ADORN

Loving you nearly split me in two.

Will you ever give me the time to mourn you?

Are you being sustained from my dreams alone?

Was I supposed to be the remedy?

Sorry I was broken too.

22

GETTING OVER YOU ISN'T EASY

I'm trying.

Is it weird that when I come to realize that you hadn't crossed my mind for longer periods of time that I get sad? Part of me doesn't ever want to move on. Part of me thinks that loving you is so lovely and I'd rather drown in this feeling than leave.

But there's another part that knows this will get easier. Whether it's me getting used to the pain or finding someone new. There's part of me that knows this emptiness is all in my head because you never filled the void to begin with.

I poured my all into another person

I gave so much time and effort and words and thoughts and prayers and love into a boy who came back into my life just to leave again.

And the part of myself that thinks that loving you is so lovely would gladly do this all over again.

But the part that feels empty is the part that knows I wouldn't make it out alive if I had to do this all over again.

If loving you was so lovely,

then leaving you alone should be heaven.

21

AND WHEN THE DAY IS DONE

Today was easier and I deserve all the credit.

I woke up and I made my bed, I didn't eat till five

But I lived.

And I didn't think once about any boy I thought I loved.

I didn't dwell on the hole in my chest.

I couldn't feel the dread that usually follows me throughout the day.

I carry so many feelings with me everywhere about everything for no good reason at all.

It felt good to not have those heavy feelings.

It felt good to be present and awake.

Here's to hoping for more days like this.

21

AND WHEN THE PAIN NEVER STOPS

I lost so much time trying to be someone who you could love.

I neglected my favorite parts of myself to become someone you would want.

It's like I learned a language I never spoke and lost any meaning to my words.

It's like I've breathed air my whole life and inhaled smoke just to be with you.

And the thing that I've struggled to make peace with as I grow older is learning to not put the blame on either of us.

I can't blame you for not feeling how I did.

And I can't blame myself for feeling anything at all.

This is me breaking the cycle.

This is me understanding what it means to be human.

To think the world revolves around me and my feelings and getting dizzy when I find out it doesn't.

21

AND WHEN THE TREES BLOOM WHITE

I loved you and you loved me and it was the biggest relief.

I meant everything I had written to you.

My love for you overshadowed any grief I had felt for you.

Everything happened exactly how it was supposed to.

If I had gotten everything I had hoped for with you

I wouldn't have been able to handle it.

I wouldn't have been able to keep you and keep my sanity when things started to fall apart.

But how lovely it was to know the truth.

You loved me and I loved you and it was the biggest relief.

22

JUST KNOW I LOVE YOU

I had realized how much I had simply missed talking to you and seeing your face in person.

I had missed you so much and also realized at that moment that trying to get rid of any feelings I had for you was futile.

They were always there. I never stopped.

And in that moment I was willing to accept anything you'd trust me enough to give, relationship, friendship, never talking to me again. It didn't matter, just know I love you enough to make it happen.

22

(Getting over you isn't easy
and when the day is done
and the pain never stops
and when the trees bloom white
just know I love you)

BUTTERFLY

An unsent letter.

From the boy who began these incessant thoughts. To the man you will one day become, for it is my biggest regret is that it will not be me who will see you grow. But it's my biggest pride, knowing whatever you strive to achieve, will burn in full brightness, with no interference from my destructive ways. I could write you a farewell. One in which I tell you all of these bottled up feelings. But out of fear of both rejection or acceptance. I cannot. For I would only hold you back. You don't need to have this on your mind as well.

So this is it.

After seven years.

And past the point of no return.

We met at a crossroads.

And I let you go first.

This time I did not follow.

I wish you nothing

but happiness in the world.

To my first love,

my heart,

my muse.

Thank you for the ocean of heartbreak,

the years of butterflies.

And the piles of poetry.

May we meet in another lifetime.

One in which you love me,

As much as I love you.

IN HATE

MATERNAL PLIGHT

It's hard to hate someone
who used to spoon feed you love.

15

RETURN TO SENDER

A story in which you rant about life and you make me cry in the grocery store at 11 PM.

It's always me, you know? It's always me that you talk to. And it's always you that you talk about. You pick sides. Yours is always right. Hers is wrong. And I couldn't agree with you more. Because if I don't, you're going to turn it around in some crazy way and try to make me feel guilty for what I think. It has been this way for as long as I can remember. I can never plead my case, or get a word inedgewise, because you're always talking over me. You continued to remind me of the things I already knew.

So when I broke down crying in the produce section of the grocery store at damn near midnight, you had the audacity to ask me what's wrong. You tell me these things almost once a month, It's like checking the mailbox and seeing a reminder to breathe. It's something you don't need to be reminded of, and yet some people feel the need to tell you to do so. You've been drilling this into my head since I was ten years old.

And I just want to tell you that I know. I know all too well. My head isn't up my ass or under a rock or even in the clouds. I know and understand crystal clear about what you're saying, even without your monthly reminder of the kind of person she really is.

I think about her every minute of every day, it's just constantly on repeat in my head that she isn't here.

16

A.G.LEDESMA

Being

a

present-

-day-

-poet

sucks

ass.

17

THE WAGER: AN ANGRY UNRESTRAINED LETTER

But I always wondered, if you knew the outcome of the baby you brought into this world in the spring of 2000, if you knew how she'd grow up to hate herself, and write poetry painting everyone else as the bad guys because she's projecting the loss of the mother figure in her life, and the rest of the childhood she didn't get the opportunity to have. If you knew that she would suffer so much day in and day out with depression, insecurities and anxiety. Would you take the extra precaution?

Or do you see something in me that I'm not seeing?

17

LIZARD

Can this finally be the year
that we stop telling people they're fat
as if they were unaware of it?

Can this be the year
that others accept my body?
For I already have.

I've always been
on the bigger side of life,
and it hasn't hindered
my way of living
a life like anybody else.

It's hard to love your body,
when society says you shouldn't.

And what benefit did you really get
from fat shaming a 17 year old girl?

DON'T SKIP AHEAD

There was a shift in my life where I stopped writing about love.

And that is just another side effect of depression.

This book stopped being about love and more about the possibility of me sticking around or not.

And I hate it.

I hate that depression has taken over, I hate that I was vulnerable enough to let it happen. I hate how one day I'm on top of the world, in love, unafraid and so painstakingly beautiful.

Then the next, I can't even find it within myself to get out of bed.

I used to sing. I used to laugh until my face was red, my stomach hurt and I couldn't breathe. I used to write about love.

This book stopped being about the journey of an unrequited love and became the tellings of falling into the clutches of depression.

Are you scared to get to the end as I am?

18

CASPIAN

Maybe I will never experience the joy of loving you.
I'm sorry.
I have no regrets for anything
 I've done for my little sisters.
But I'm already exhausted.

I always wanted to be a mom.

22

SCHADENFREUDE

I wonder how much stress my parents would be under
if I acted like them when they were my age.

I wonder how much stress they would be under
if they actually knew everything I've done.

Everyday I'm thankful that reading minds isn't a thing.

16

THE BULL AND THE MAIDEN

And yet another piece of you has died tonight.

Going through life knowing the exact moment
Where everything changed and everything went wrong
You acknowledged it then
and you acknowledge it now
That your life wasn't going to remain the same.

You died that night too.

19

PHANTOM DEPARTURE

Whatever it is you're about to say,
I'm not prepared for any of it.

Because when someone
who you only talk to on occasion
Messages you out of the blue
Saying that we need to talk
It's never good.

A hundred possible reasons
are running through my head as to what it could be
And each one is more devastating than the next.

18

(I never thought I'd be scared to see my mother.)

"JUST STOP BEING SAD"

You've got your whole life ahead of you.
And life is just filled with periods,
phases and fragments
but none of them last unbearable amounts of time
unless you will them to.
If you will yourself to be sad,
then nothing good will come your way
because you were too busy being sad.

It's not the end of the world,
It's just the beginning of a new one.

16

SATURN

You give someone the best parts of yourself
only to have them leave.

It's like one day I woke up and you weren't there.

14

(When sharing isn't caring.)

STEEL RIB CAGE AND A PORCELAIN HEART

I cry a lot.

And I'm not saying that to be relatable and funny,

I actually mean that I cry *A LOT.*

I cry when I'm happy, mad, frustrated, confused.

I mostly cry for no damn reason at all

and I hate it because I can never

place myself in the mood of *content.*

I'm not satisfied with content

I'm not satisfied with myself.

17

KALEIDOSCOPIC

I say that I have nothing left to say on the matter,
but me saying that contradicts everything.

Your presence hits me harder than your absence.
What hurts the most is that
there's nothing I could do to stop this.

16
(I was not enough for you to stay.)

CONDITION OF THE HEART

One of these days you're going to reach out to me
and I'm not going to be there.
I don't want to miss you.
So I'm going to make you miss me instead.

15

COPACETIC

I wasn't allowed the opportunity to explode
into the world exactly what I wanted to say.

I was like a stick of TNT
being held close to lit flames,
being tempted to spark.

I wasn't allowed to combust because
I have everyone's secrets under my tongue.

17

CHUTZPAH

I could only sit here and wish that I could tell you
how hard this has been for me.

That each day that I walk out of those doors
and I see your car waiting for me,
my heart drops to my stomach in absolute dread.

I don't want to keep your secrets anymore.

18

PROSELYTE

Because one day all of the sudden we weren't able to talk to each other like we used to. And one day out of nowhere you became the most discouraging person in my life. No longer my biggest supporter, you chose her then proceeded to tell me that she's not permanent.

I'm tired of the people in my life choosing temporary people over me. I'm tired of staying long enough to let it get to this point.

How could you say to let the storm pass when I'm already under?

18

ATLAS

Gravity betrayed me as it grasped the tears
from my eyes and presented them to you.
I look up when I'm about to cry.
I look up and pray that I don't.

12

CLAUSTROPHOBIA OF THE SOUL

Something happened to my relationship with my parents when I was in high school. It's supposed to be common to drift away from them during that time, but I began to resent them for my own issues that I couldn't solve on my own.

Something happened in between the time of my junior year and senior year after I had finally begun to come clean about my depression that I grew closer to my dad only for things to fall apart again.

I internalized a hatred I didn't know could exist, I bore a grudge for things that were out of my control. It was like claustrophobia in my soul. Because it's not normal to be this angry all the time. It stunts your growth.

19

MATTER

The worst relationship in my life was never human.
The worst relationship has always been
 and will always be food.

I gorge myself to forget.
I starve myself to feel.

And my poor body
had to suffer the consequences of it all.

22

DE NOVO

You may not ever lie to us,
but that doesn't mean you tell the truth.

You made her the sinner
While you became the martyr

Growing up is realizing how
human your parents really are

And that their calamities passed down from
Their own parents will one day become our own.

22

GROWING THROUGH THIS

Would you fully understand me when I tell you my parents were children too?

That my dad has been a father longer than he hasn't?

That my mother loved me long before she even knew how to?

That I was aware of these struggles before I could even make sense of it all?

Have you ever been told your existence was an accident before you reached the age of five?

Did you go to kindergarten with soiled underwear and a lighter in your pocket?

And in spite of it all, my biggest wish is to be reborn as my mother's mother so that she could finally feel maternal love.

And to become Atlas for my father and carry all his stress and burdens so he could get a moment's rest. To burn his work uniforms to ash and lock him in the house and force him to sleep so that he could actually dream for the first time in years.

Let me feel this pain for us all.

Let me show you what your love has become of me.

22

IN SORROW

FELICITY

How do you explain your unhappiness to the people you love dearly? How can you just tell them you've been suffering and floating along the river of life face down, feeling like you can't come up for air?

I can't seem to ever speak a word about what troubles me. Mostly because the people in my life don't make the effort to listen.

Would they just assume it's a phase? Something that will just take time to get over? More clutter to stuff under the rug?

I am drowning among a sea of people, but I don't speak a word because in my head I know there are others who have it worse than me. But telling myself constantly for years that my problems... That my *depression* was nothing to worry about, it was six years later I finally realized that *"nothing"* at some point in time turned into something. It became hard to get out of bed in the morning. I found myself looking for any opportunity for an escape. Some good. Most bad. I've thought about taking my own life on many occasions. Things felt as if they weren't going to change. Hell, as I'm writing this right now I still don't feel as if things are okay. There's no bright side. Nor was there any feeling of love towards my muse.

This monstrosity known as depression had stripped me of my being. And the things I loved most in the world suddenly became the things that I loathed. My mother. My father. My muse. My fucking life. But being chronically depressed is what led my pen to paper. And suddenly it's no longer just an attempt at trying to make myself happy, suddenly it's losing something that has become a part of me.

How do you let something go when it was what dragged you through the long days. Kept you company through the nights, and held your hand through the tears?

How do you explain to your loved ones that your unhappiness is what brought a formation of sickly-sweet words... And that you would relinquish your felicity just for the sake of some normalcy?

16

(This was the first time I wrote the word depression.

This was the first time I admitted to myself I wasn't happy.

How weird that a page of words helped me to understand and overcome so much)

LITTLE BY LITTLE

There's going to be a time in your life
when you're going to decide
That bare minimum isn't enough.

Is it that time yet?

11

HYSTERICAL

The only way to prove that you have a heart: *Break it.*

Turning stone hearts to flesh,

Make the ice queen combust.

Cry until someone notices.

For these are all things you can manage.

12

REAGAN

"I'm not going to waste my time being sorry anymore."

(You said this when you gave me a ride home one night and although I do poke fun at you for it, It actually helped me. We're both highkey messed up, but we both somehow found the humor in it all.

Thank you for making me laugh even when I felt like I never could again.)

MEDUSA

My thighs as I sit, expand.
Surpassing the chair I am in.

He once told me, *"There's just so much of you to love."*
And my stupid, insecure self, Took that as an insult.
I hated my capsule before I could ever even begin to love it.

I saw my stretch marks as a sign of weakness.
Because if counted up you could see

How many times she said she'll visit.
How many times he didn't notice me.
How many nights I cried myself to sleep.

Because I learned at an early age
That it's easier to stuff your face
Then face your demons.

17

NOVEMBER

How long did we lie there,
In each other's company
Lying to ourselves?

How long was it
until we were forced
to face the truth?

The sun came and passed.
And so did you.

And in solitude
I stood at the mouth of the river,
Thinking of you.

I don't know how many times
I've fought this damn current.
The relentless waves,
The ups and downs.

Fighting for air,
Fighting to live,
Fighting for you.

And in solitude
I stood at the mouth of the river,
And I jumped.

And I can't swim.

13

GIRL ALMIGHTY

The day you came,
Suddenly the world
had its hold on me.

You gave me
a reason to stay.

But I'll take the credit
For continuing on,
Even when I didn't want to.

I'll give you the credit,
For making my heart
Beat a mile a minute.

You gave me a reason to stay,
But I gave myself 1,000 more.

And I deserve the credit
because this shit is hard.

14

SHOGUN

"I wanna enjoy tomorrow."

-Dad

16

(Although these aren't words directly from you, they were from a page of blackout poetry I had you do. And you asked if they always had to be sad and when I said no, you gave me a colorful page back. You indulged in something very close to my heart, poetry. And all the while you showed me there can be light in what I write. I've written many thanks you's over the years and tons of comical birthday cards, but I don't think I could ever fully put into words how much I look up to you. And I live everyday knowing I will never be as fearless as you.)

THE PEAK

I was always playing a part.

And I don't know how many times

I had to sit back and see each life I was leading.

Half of them are hidden away.

From the girl who had everything together,

Because half a million people depended on her for it.

To a school smart girl

Who's future outshined her darkest nights.

Each part is expected to do great things.

But the part that writes this

Is projected to be *dead*

Within the next five years.

16

AGE OF UNREASONING

Because at the age of 12 you had the wish to die

And at the age of 18 you had the wish to live

You've come to terms with the fact that

You were born middle aged

And you shed years off

Rather than grow.

18

HOW DO YOU TELL YOUR THOUGHTS TO FUCK OFF?

"If most of my anxiety stems
from the fear of not having
anything constant in my life,
maybe death is the right choice."

16

(What went through my head
after I told my therapist I wasn't suicidal,
because sometimes we lie out of fear.
Fear of opening a new can of worms
and realizing how far you haven't come.)

NOTE TO SELF:

I am scatterbrained
and ready for death
but I'm not ready for dying.

17

BACKWARDS

I set my expectations too high.

And yet you're restless.

Why is it that I can last months without eating,
but only eleven days without sleeping?

11

COME BACK TO EARTH

The hardest thing in life
that I've had to stomach
in my short existence,
is listening to people
telling me to wait
for things to get better.

18

BRAKETHROUGH

And in the end, I had realized
that the only reason there was self-suffering
was because I dwelled on present problems
rather than looking at the big picture.

And then I realized that life is so short
and yet so long at the same time.
And I just had to know
that these feelings would pass.

And I had to accept the fact
that I'm just a small spec
in the timeline of the world,
and even if I don't become a legend,
doesn't mean I didn't matter.

18

ODE TO ELIOT

"Do I dare disturb the universe?"

Because in recent light love isn't kind.
It's actually quite daft.

And you have to be secure enough in yourself
to even begin to entertain the thought
That someone could ever love someone
As needy as I

18

LARVA

I love you so much and I'll try to be there for you
as much as I can.

I want you to know that you were the brightest thing
to happen to me in the darkest time of my life.
You were a gift through all this mess,
and I'd go through it all again for you.

I am so incredibly thankful for you.

17

IN WHICH THINGS GO DOWN, AGAIN

I didn't think I was going to live to see my 16th birthday,
let alone taking a driver's test or graduating high school.

I didn't plan for 16
Nor did I plan for the rest of my life.

And now I'm faced with wanting to live,
And having to catch up
To a future I thought wasn't possible.

Two months till 18
And I am prepared for nothing.

I have already failed
Before I even began.
And I'm sorry.

But sometimes I think
That I was supposed to stop at 16.

18

MARCH NUMB

I've hit the stage in my depression
where it's easier to hide it.

I always thought the peak of my depression
Was when I was a sobbing mess
that couldn't stop being sad.

But it turns out the peak
is when you feel nothing.

I am so numb
And so good at hiding it.

Every conversation lost its meaning.
Every smile is forced.

I don't even remember the last time
I laughed until my stomach hurt.

I'm just going through the motions,
Being upturned to the river of life
Floating on a liferaft as its currents try to tip me
But because I've lost all sight of direction,
I don't even know if I'm actually drowning.

DAWN OF DIVINITY

What a symbolic thing.

That each time you cross a threshold,

Your life is going to be altered in some way.

Was I heading for disaster,

or was I going to walk out of here

feeling more appreciative of my life?

17

(When I opened the door to the church
where my therapy sessions would be held.)

ALONE WITH ROSS

The world has always just consisted
of black and white for me.
There were just long periods of good times
and long periods of bad times.

There was never once just a fucking middle ground
for me to catch my bearings on,
there was never a place for me to fit in.
That mix of colors,
that gray,
was always over ruled by the dark.

That's where I always find myself over and over again.
Just a jumble of tears and swearing.
And why do I just let it fucking happen?
Why was I always just leaving myself unhappy or unsatisfied?

15

JUVENILITY

Depression became a norm,
and suddenly all hangouts became pity parties,
laughter ceased and we all questioned aloud
if continuing on was actually worth it.

It's like depression became
the fourth person in my group of friends,
Very much uninvited and unwelcome.
I want the good times back,
So fuck off already.

(When on a saturday night we stay indoors crying
about things we have no control over)

ONE-HUNDRED AND EIGHTY DEGREES

It was the belief that this feeling would last forever that led me towards my downward spiral of not exactly crying, nor raging or anything really. Just an unexplainable pain of existence, as if gravity took its toll on me. It was the fact that this mental pain brought forth physical trauma as well as an unexplainable need for isolation is most likely the reason why my brain has come to a complete halt, eliminating emotional ties and throwing me into the void.

I am numb.

There were a lot of nights where I asked no one *"When is this going to end?"*, *"Will I ever not be depressed?"*, *"Do I even want to wake up tomorrow?"* And *"Can you please make this stop?"* Gradually I stopped crying every night. I stopped getting angry at myself. I stopped getting scared to interact with people (mostly because I didn't leave the house to do so) but along with all the bad, I lost the good too. I lost to my own demons and I didn't even know it until I hit the bottom of the abyss I'd like to call the peak of my depression. I thought the peak of my depression was when I was crying myself to sleep at night because I couldn't get my brain to shut up. I thought the peak was when I was home alone and I would look at myself in the bathroom mirror and unwillingly scream all of my anger out trying to release some of this inner turmoil I seem to have plenty of. I thought the peak was the absolute dread I would feel in the pit of my stomach knowing that I was going to be in a crowded place for longer than I'd like. But the peak was when I stopped feeling those things.

I stopped feeling everything.

I thought it was progress. I thought that I had finally gotten past the worst of it only to come to find out that this was just the peak. This was when spending time with my grandma, the one person who makes me the happiest person on this planet, suddenly didn't. I had started to make excuses for not wanting to leave the house. And I just watched as my grades dropped and all the missing assignments piled up. I hated the confusion everyone felt because that was something I didn't typically struggle with, but I was frustrated because how could they not have known then? The endless back talk, the stupidity of my outbursts and failure to keep fighting is something I will always be ashamed of. Trying to find relief through reckless means, all those nights I was home alone, my loved ones trusting me to not do anything stupid, their trust was misplaced on multiple occasions. It still baffles me as to how I am still alive.

Now that I am afloat, I can breathe and see all too clearly. I would like to apologize for taking this life for granted. I would also like to tell all these invisible demons I'm battling to kindly fuck off and never come back. And I would like to personally thank everyone who stayed through my collapse, and those who will help with my rebuilding.

There's a lot of bad shit in this world, but there's so many good things too. It's strange that the smallest things are what really kept me fighting. Any night my dad and I would come home late, as we would walk inside I would look up to see the stars and it grounded me every time. And each morning when I would see the sky turn pink I knew it meant that I had made it another day, the sunrise always let me know I was still alive. And anytime my little sister laughed, I would forget how awful I was feeling because seeing the world through her eyes made everything so much brighter.

Find people, things and reasons to chase the darkness away, live for them.

Live your life in spite of depression.

LOTUS

Isn't it crazy how someone can suffer for so long
and have nobody know about it?

That my silence, mood swings and lack of motivation
is just perceived as an epidemic to teendom?

Emotions, feelings and disorders don't really matter until I'm
dead

15

LINGUAPHILE

I don't know how to make this shit poetic anymore.
I'm so tired of living.

19

TIMOROUS

I should go to sleep but I'm just so happy right now and I don't want that to go away. I have a great guy that gives me lots of attention. I had parent teacher conferences, and all of my teachers told my dad about how hard I work. My teacher even said that there's so many things I could end up doing in life and that she's excited to see what venture I pick. It's both nice and scary that there are people that have these ideals for my future, She said that she feels like I'm going to do something big one day and sometimes I have enough hope that I feel that way too.

I don't want to go to sleep because tomorrow all of this could change

Tomorrow my boy could decide I'm high maintenance and drop me, tomorrow I could fail a test, tomorrow my dad could suddenly decide that he's tired of taking care of me. Tomorrow I could throw my whole life away.

I can't sleep because tomorrow I might want to kill myself again.

So here's to staying in today.

Staying in right now.

Here's to the feeling of the present

and the fear of tomorrow.

Goodnight and I'm sorry.

19

RELAPSE

How is it that I'm not used to this pain yet?
Each morning as I wake up
it hits me just as hard as it did the first time.

18

GROUND CONTROL TO MAJOR TOM

I'm on the verge of breaking down every fucking minute.

I don't know how things got so shitty so fast.

I have no plan

But I'm going to fight like hell.

19

WHEN SILENCE BECOMES A KILLING MACHINE

Becoming a victim of my own mind was the plot twist in my life.

18

(This pain needed to be felt.
This life needed to be lived.
These words needed to be written.
I'm still here.)

IT WAS DIAL SOAP IF YOU WANTED TO KNOW

The sorrow dug a deep hole in my chest that I didn't know how to fill. Then as time went on rather than trying to fill it with temporary things I just gave up and the only thing I did with my life was wait for it to end.

I danced with death three times in my life. I did it with tears in my eyes, love on my mind and surrender in my soul. I did it because I felt like there was nothing left. Hope was a word that had lost its meaning. Faith was something I was missing, and a conversation was what I needed.

When I was at my worst, I would lie awake at night clutching a bar of soap in my hand. Ever since I was little, I had been drawn to clean smells. It was like the four-year-old in me was the one who was trying to hold me together, it was like she was the one who kept me from breaking. I smelled that bar of soap until my nose burned, my head hurt, and I could see the sun rise. The longest I went without sleep medicated on a bar of soap was 5 and a half days. That was the least I've felt alive.

There's a lot of things I don't say. There's still more to learn, more to reveal about me. I'm sorry things are coming out right now, but I guess I'm finally ready for people to know just what has happened to me.

19

SURRENDER

I've been fighting against myself
for the past eight years.

18

CRISE DE NERFS

Broken people raise broken children
who spend the majority of their lives
Trying to weld themselves together again.

I still crave normalcy in my life
Only getting bits and pieces of it
as I stay here with you.

18

(I accidentally welded onto you)

IN WHICH I LOSE HOPE

If I'm being honest,

I'm always going to be going through some shit.

So when I say I'm fine,

just know I'm a damn liar

and I'm so fucking sorry I'm not better yet

18

(I've been going to therapy for a fucking year
and I just feel like I've been moving backwards.)

CROCODILE

I know it must've been hard to try to help me with my future when I didn't even try.

I thank God for your persistence, because I would be nowhere without you.

18

(You're my favorite.)

RHINE RIVER

It's been almost a year since we've talked or hung out,
And if someone would've told me that a year ago
I would've died at the thought.

I never would've thought that one day
when I looked to my side you wouldn't be there.
There's no hard feelings,
We didn't have a fight,
There was just *nothing*.

And I guess that's the part that hurts.
That we both did nothing to keep this going.

I guess it was just our time.
People change and grow.
Sometimes apart.

19

MINUTE BY MINUTE

Nothing worse than reading a story with a bad ending.

It's the meanest thing an author could do.

But it's also the most satisfying

because it leaves them questioning.

The story stays with them, and in their hearts,

they hope that their own story won't end badly.

16

(When I thought the end was near.)

THE DAY THE EARTH OPENED UP AND SWALLOWED ME WHOLE

At the age of thirteen when most of my friends wrote in their diaries about their parents not buying them new things or crushes on boys that didn't even care for them, I was writing out a list of grievances and how much I had wanted to die. My depression aged me beyond what my classmates were going through, and I have to say that is one of the things I hate the most. I wish I could go back to the day where I went too far to reach.

I wish I could go back to the day the earth opened up and swallowed me whole.

I wish younger me never had to suffer through such feelings.

19

FRANCINE ROBIN

A thousand hearts beat for you now.

12

TIME I'VE WASTED

I don't think I ever could've predicted this path for me. Because in life we always look forward to the good, the prospects of a happy life are the reasons that we all keep going. But we never stopped to think that your greatest downfalls are just around the corner.

My younger self wanted nothing more than to be an adult. But if I'm being 100% honest, turning18 was one of the worst things to happen to me.

Living past the date that I thought was my expiration is exasperating. Because I still feel that I should have perished that day. Now I wake up to a rotten life.

18

BRIGHT EYES, WEAK STOMACH

You will never truly be content with your life
Or you're never going to know when your peak is
because you spent that time believing
that you'd always go up.

16

(The melody in my sixteen year old brain.)

IPSO FACTO

The older I get I do more of the things
I promised myself I wouldn't do.
The older I get I witness more of the sacrifices
the people in my life make.

I live with the most selfless people in the world.
And I show thanks by writing shitty poems.

I'm sorry and incredibly thankful.

18

SI JE SUIS MORT JEUNE

One does wish for happiness and bliss

As one cries from sorrow and goodbyes.

Had I known myself from today

I would not have wished myself away.

A year ago felt like yesterday.

To bring back the past and a life lived too fast.

To know what you know now, then, a gift an end;

The madness pauses,

holding back from all these awful causes.

Growing, changing, rearranging.

Life lessons, mixed blessings.

Everything happens for a reason.

Past seasons show there's nowhere to go,

You now know more than you ever knew then.

Time passed too fast, an end.

YOUNG GUNS

Sometimes it's just really funny how chronic depression works with me.

I forget that just because it's gone

doesn't mean it won't come back

and I spend those peaks thinking

I'd never come down.

I made a bad habit of holding onto things

for too long in every aspect of my life.

I horde physically and mentally.

I keep people in my life that told me

they'd never hurt me.

I fall in love with people that don't want me.

I set myself up for these heartbreaks

Then have the audacity to ask why I'm hurting?

It's funny how chronic depression works with me

And that it's never really gonna go away.

As time goes on I'm just going to find

New ways to live with it.

New ways to lie about it.

New ways to die with it.

19

THERAPY WORKS, JUST NOT FOR ME

I couldn't even be myself in front of someone who was paid to help me.

19

IN WHICH I DIDN'T READ THE TERMS AND CONDITIONS

Nobody told me there were going to be days
Where I didn't want to exist.

There wasn't precaution to depression.
I couldn't really take steps to avoid it.
Once it has you it doesn't really leave.
And that's the hardest thing to wrap my mind around.

Because the days that I'm up
I wonder how I was ever down,
And the days that I'm down
I tell myself that up was a false comfort.

I'm always going to have this as a part of my life.
But it's up to me to decide whether to take control or not.
And try as I might,
The current is far too strong.
To continuously fight.

It's hard to keep faith
When you've lost your compass
The storms rolls through
and you're too exhausted to even stay afloat.

REACHING IN, SPEAKING OUT AND NOTICING

A new heartbreak I've come to realize
I wasn't myself for months
And no one had noticed

The burning of a man isn't apparent
until you can't stand the smell of his charred flesh
Even then you just walk away to get away from it
Or hope enough time passes that he's turned to dust.

I could've died a thousand and one times
And still been unhappy
Had I not let embers escape

Misactions are just as daunting
Silence is just as damaging

19

HOW MANY TIMES WILL I RELAPSE BEFORE THE DECADE'S OVER?

In hindsight,

Maybe I deserve this.

Maybe I did something wrong

and now all these tears,

dark thoughts and sleepless nights are a repercussion.

Whatever it was that I did, *I'm sorry.*

I would take it all back

If it meant I didn't have to feel pain like this.

19

DROWNING IN BUBBLES

I often think about, what if I hadn't won?

It's been a rough couple of months and I keep thinking, *"this is going to be it, this is going to be the worst thing that happened to me at 18,"* but things keep getting wild. The end of this little world my dad has attempted to construct for me is hanging by a thread and within two months I'm going to be on my own. I'm going to start a new chapter and I'm going to be ending this one.

This chapter is where I've fallen in love, recklessly endangering my heart, this is the chapter that my mother left too soon. This is the chapter where friendships fell apart and I learned that people tend to grow apart and go their own way. This is the chapter where I learned that my parents are human too, they make mistakes, and I can't control them but just communicate what I need and hope they understand. I learned that boys aren't magically going to fix every part of me. I learned that I have a tendency to overthink things and that each time I've taken a chance despite my anxiety I've been successful.

I learned that I'm going to be okay.

I'm not going to miss this part of my life,

I know that for sure.

But I am going to miss my youth.

18

MINUTIAE

Yesterday was 2 years ago since I've told people about my depression,

and yesterday two years ago, I was listening to *Adele*, trying to calm down because I felt like the world was ending.

Yesterday in the present I went to the lake with my sisters and my nephew and I watched dumb movies with Erika and we laughed and screamed so hard.

I know I do this a lot where I have the tendency to prioritize remembering dates. But it's because there was a time when I didn't value anything,

There was a time when I thought I was out of time.

19

GO TO SLEEP YOU'RE DREAMING

This thing comes in waves.

The first stages of what I was feeling as a teenager were manageable. I cried a lot but knew how to calm myself down. I was restless but I always knew when I was awake.

Now that I'm in my 20s I can't tell the difference between living and dreaming.

I can't cry anymore.

I can feel the hole in my chest.

Food makes me sick.

I know this is bad and for once I can feel the fear creeping in.

I get dizzy just from thinking.

And I overthink. I overthink. I overthink.

I laugh at things that aren't even remotely funny, and once I start laughing I realize how much I miss the feeling and try to keep laughing.

Holding on.

Letting go, letting go. Feeling nothing.

22

5150

From an absence that caused tidal waves.
I kept seeing constellations where only stars existed.
I'm still floating. Still no clue as to where.
I was flooded with sorrow.
Drowning in both the good and the bad.
It's only horrific because I can't feel either.

It's only horrific because I'd rather feel pain
than feel nothing at all.

I'm still floating.

17

FOUNTAIN OF YOUTH

Sometimes I get so lost in trying to help
That I can't see when I'm being used.

I give so much of myself
Taking now feels like sin.

Sometimes I feel like I'm living in someone else's body. Or that I've already lived this life and I'm being forced to sit through it again.

It's too much and yet too little. I'm wide awake yet exhausted. It's black or it's white and never gray here. No middle ground between my emotions. And when there is a middle ground it's numbness. It's me trying not to feel either.

I remember being in New York City when I was at an Italian restaurant in Times Square cheers-ing to my aunt and grandma with tears in my eyes because I stayed alive long enough to see that dream through. I remember thinking to myself *"this is probably the happiest I'm ever going to be"* And I was simultaneously hit with the pain that I would never experience that moment again.

I was already mourning a moment that hadn't passed. And I wish I didn't do that.

19

EVERGREEN

Because in life you want things to happen quickly. You want to get to the good parts, you want to fast forward through all the hardships, the heartbreaks and the bullshit. But you don't get to appreciate the good parts without all of the bad.

I'll wait as long as it takes.

And if it wasn't meant to be, I'll know.

And I'll be okay.

16

I'LL BE SEEING YOU

How is my family going to cope with losing me
when I'm leaving a messy room behind.

16

(My depression room is so bad
I'd be embarrassed to end my life here.)

TUNNEL VISION AND BIRDS-EYE VIEW

How do I save me from myself?

Some days it's like tunnel vision, like I know the world I'm experiencing is from my point of view but everything seems smaller and less significant.

Everything seems easier to lose. And I care less to keep trying.

Other days it's like I'm ultra zoomed out, like I'm looking down on myself from above, that I'm being horrified with how I feel and think and live. That I feel bad for myself.

It feels like I wanna be better. Like I'm on the mend.

How do I save me from myself when I can't even bear the sight of my own sorrow?

How do I fix these broken parts without losing myself?

I could go to therapy again and pull someone else through the same incessant cycle.

Of tunnel vision and bird's eye view. Of feeling sorry or feeling nothing. I could explain to someone else that not waking up tomorrow would probably be beneficial to my mental health.

Or I could take the suppressors and feel nothing even worse. I could take them and exist and live pretending that I'm living this life with goals and expectations and that I'm waiting on good things to come.

Or I could continue doing nothing and continue having the only thing I do with my life is wait for it to end.

I could keep neglecting this capsule.

I could keep running on empty.

But I can't keep scaring my family.

I don't want to pretend to want to exist.

2020

Ever since October I felt like I've been reeling and stumbling. February was a punch in the gut, it always is. March was like a movie. April was like a living nightmare. May was hope and June is like acid rain. I started biting my nails again… A sign of relapse. A sign of failure. A sign of worse things to come. I've been losing large amounts of hair. A sign of stress. Evidence of my hourly panic. Everytime someone messages me I get nauseous and terrible chest pains. It's PTSD. It's crazy how often I've been fucked over by a text message. How many times things had to be typed rather than spoken as to break me from miles away rather than in person. Messages like those are what make me fear every notification that comes through my phone. My phone is like a tumor. I've attached it to myself and made it malignant. It connects me to the world and disconnects me from reality. It's a sign of my age. I'm 20. I'm 20 and I've already thought about dying more times than I could count. That's the side effect of being selfish. That's the side effect to thinking that subtracting yourself from the picture would break the equation completely but it doesn't. The world will still turn regardless of broken hearts. It will still turn and I will be dust. But right now I'm alive just waiting to see what will happen next. I'll be dust when it's time to be dust. July was frigid. August was freedom. September is hell, I wanted to be dust in September…

20

GIVE ME SOME TIME TO FIND A REASON TO STAY. (I'LL STAY)

Going deeper and deeper into something I won't make it out of.

Writing these, praying to God I'm too much of a coward to have it see the light of day.

I've written so many goodbyes knowing these words

could never be enough to heal the damage I've caused.

Going back and forth between loving this life and wanting an escape.

I'll stay.

I'll wake up each tomorrow and keep searching for my reason.

I'll engage with the world and keep my heart open.

I am worthy of love and life.

I am worthy of happiness and content.

22

APOLOGIA

APOLOGIA

Technically an apologia is supposed to be a formal defense of an opinion. But I'm not defending this work in any way, this is just me apologizing for how long this took me to put this out into the world. Friends and family haven't heard me shut up about this project since 2015. I felt it was slightly necessary to add further gratitude beyond the dedication at the beginning of this book. I have so many people in my life that throughout these years didn't add grief to all my suffering. I've been surrounded by so much love and kindness and patience. Maybe I'll never be able to truly convey this all but here's me trying. So many of you are the reason this book came into existence and this will be the first thank you of many: *Thank you.*

To my grade school love that sparked this whole mess, I'll probably email you the manuscript of this just to let you know how much my sanity depended on you when I was ten. Hell it depended on you until I was fifteen. I still see you around to this day and you don't trip my heart up as much as you used to. But it was one hell of a crush I had on you. Inspired a lot of shitty poems. Actually every crush that I ever wrote about in this book… Was it obvious? Did you guys ever notice the chubby girl who'd make an embarrassing effort to be near you?

To my high school peers and teachers for knowing about this book for months and only minimally teasing me about it. To my high school marketing teacher Mrs. George, whom I spent a majority of my time with, sophomore through senior year. One day when I was supposed to be there for an after school event, I stood outside your classroom because you were in a meeting with a bunch of fancy people but I heard you talking about me. Usually when I eavesdrop I walk away with a broken heart, but you sat in front of all those fancy people and told them about my potential. You told them about this poetry book and I'd like to credit you for giving these words a genre. You said, "She writes some kind of… Trauma poetry?"

To Mr.Swalley for flipping me off in class when I spaced out and for helping me find the humor in the crappy parts of my life. It felt good to laugh about these situations instead of constantly crying. Going to your guy's classes was so much better than being at home. Thanks for giving me that space where I felt like I could breathe. Thanks for helping me visualize my potential.

To Chad, I met you at a state DECA competition my senior year of high school. You handed me your business card and told me you wanted to be the first one to buy my book after sitting through my mock business proposal about it. People like you are what make the world go round, and if I didn't have that interaction with you this would've never seen the light of day because I just wasn't sure if it was something that would be of value to the general public. Thanks Chad, keep doing what you're doing. Keep being that encouraging voice, because you might just be the only one that supports these ideas.

To my Hanna. You were here for half of this book. By all circumstances we should have fallen out of touch a long time ago but by some miracle we still held on. Who knew such good things could come from One Direction and talking to a stranger on the internet (;. We have this weird way of knowing when the other is upset and a lot of crazy chances and coincidences between the two of us. Growing up and having you to talk to even when it felt like I had no one else was such a relief. Knowing you now makes every bad thing in my life suddenly worth it. You're going to be a part of my life forever, sorry but that's just how it is. I love you more than you'll ever know. I mean it.

To Reagan. It's been a long ass road and I'm so glad we've made it. I trust you with my life and you've become the guardian of my soul after years of me neglecting it. You've seen every ugly part of me, my life and yet still you stay. You make the biggest effort to include me in the little things you do and you love my sisters as if they were your own. In the eight years I've known you, you've become so much a part of my life that I don't even know what life was like before you were in it. Thanks for your patience, thanks for your love and thanks for teaching me about God.

To Carter (Barter). Is adding you here too much? I don't care, I just wanted a little space to personally thank you and to tell you I miss you. I don't know how else to put this into words other than saying thank you for being in my life. Thank you for letting me know. And thank you for never turning me away, especially when I suddenly decide to be brave. I love you loads.

AJ, my brother!! Thank you for always reaching out when you can, for being hilarious and someone I could confide in. And thank you for harassing me about publishing this book, hope you enjoyed reading this on your e-reader <3

To my family. My sisters are my light. I didn't exactly come around to appreciating my older sisters until I got older myself, but just wanted to say I'm sorry for being such a pest. I think you're the only two that could put up with my dumbass full time. To Carolyn, the eldest, the one to pioneer this broken family and taking care of me when you shouldn't have had to, thank you. Thank you for giving you your amazing music taste. You're always the leader in my life. You're an amazing mother and I'm pretty sure your son is the reason why the sun rises.

To Erika, we became best friends at the end of 2018. You once told me in a *Buffalo Wild Wings* that being with me is what healed your heart, but I also credit that to you, for me. I don't think I've ever laughed as hard with anyone else as I do with you, we constantly get asked if we're high just because of how intoxicating we are to each other. We both came together at such a bad time in our lives, which is weird to say. I hate that there was so much time lost and wasted on other people when this whole time my sister could've been my best friend? We know it now and that's all that matters.

To Brook, the Mookly Smookly, you changed pretty much every aspect of my life. I've spent 15 years being the baby of the family. Then you came and put your grubby little baby hands all over that title. Before you I was immensely sad, but when you were there I was just immensely sad with a baby to look after. You made life fun again for me and the whole family. I don't know when you'll ever come around to reading this, I wonder if you'll be reading it holographically. Anyways being with you everyday, looking after you and teaching you dumb things prevented me from doing so many bad things. Seeing the world through your eyes gave me the motivation I needed to continue living rather than just existing.

To my handsome nephew, Adriel. The Silly-Billy. You're a goon. There's so many things I'm excited for now, both you and Brooklyn just seemed to bring all the fun back into life. I want to keep you young so bad. I want every Halloween to be filled with your cute little costumes. I want every Christmas to be you getting the loudest toys. I want every Easter spent watching you miss easily hidden eggs in the backyard. I just really want you to stay little forever, but if you did you'd probably never get to read this. So Adriel, I just want you to know that I'm so thankful for how much love you give to your mother everyday. I think all children heal holes inside their parents and I see your mom when she's with you and she looks whole again and I don't think I've ever seen her as happy as she is to be with you.

To Dakota Moda. GIRL YOU WEREN'T EVEN BORN YET WHEN I FINISHED THE FIRST DRAFT OF THIS BOOK?? You middle child-ed me so hard. Thanks to Brooklyn I learned how to be a big sister and got things better the second time around. After you were born I had dropped out of college, and thank goodness you were there to take my mind off of these failing feelings. Because how can I be failing anything when my little sisters are happy and taken care of? I can't picture our family without you. You were the perfect *last* edition to this crazy family.

To my grandpa Kenny for being frank and funny at the same time. The stories you pitched to me might need a little work, but you got the right idea. We don't share blood but we do share laughs and I think that means more to me than anything else. Thank you for being my triple A and those big hugs even when I was too lazy to get up.

To my mom. These words took a long time for me to get out. And I'm sorry. My earliest memories in life are of you. Taking naps, eating pasta, pretending to be asleep so we don't have to go out into the living room and clean, your L.L. Cool J. alarm, don't let the bed bugs bite. All of it. The older I get I come to understand you better. When I was sixteen I thought my world was ending. When you were sixteen another was just beginning. And if we traded places I don't think I'd know what to do. I want nothing more in life than for you to be happy mama. I forgive you for everything and I'll love you forever.

To my dad. I wrote about your fearlessness because it's true, that is the one thing that I can never possess. You are so sure, sturdy, smart and wise. It's everything I could've asked for and more in a dad, you were like a boulder in a hurricane. The one thing I will always remember and will probably tell others about you when they ask about what kind of man my father was, I will tell them this: Even when all he wanted to do was sleep after working long hours, he stayed awake and did all that he could for us before the sun went down. That you fought exhaustion and stress just for a couple hours with us. You once told me that you don't see any of your hard labor and hours at work as a sacrifice because it's something that you wanted to do for us and from that moment on I was floored with what luck I have. One thing I hope for you to understand and carry forward is to take better care of yourself, to do more of the things that make you happy because you've spent most of your life providing for others. One day I hope to give you the world. Just wait until I can find a way to do that please.

To my grandma Carolyn. I've held off on writing this part for as long as I possibly could and also it was impossible to get through without bursting into tears every ten minutes. There's no simplistic way to convey to everyone that reads this that almost every part of my "adult" self that is finishing this project is the result of a very patient, very selfless grandmother who had given me the time and the love I needed to grow. June of 2017, I played my spoken word piece *Felicity* for you. We had just been on our way back from having dinner in Hutchinson, you had me drive out there to get more experience driving on the highway (you literally taught me how to drive.) I figured on the way back would be as good of a time as any to finally come clean about my depression. You didn't hesitate for a second to offer me help. The next day you had a doctor's appointment ready to go and within the next week you had me in therapy and for the rest of that year and a half you had paid for and drove me to these appointments that were in another town. You not only helped me salvage what little life I was planning on living, you encouraged me to go further. You got me through school. You helped me get a driver's license. You helped me get into college. These are in no way, small things. You helped me with these things that, before therapy or before talking about my depression, I had never seen becoming a reality for me. You have given me this second chance at life after I had already given up on myself. It's heart wrenching to acknowledge the compassion you have, but I gotta do this because none of this would've ever happened if it weren't for you. These words would've never seen the light of day had you decided that day in 2017, to just let me be. You're my favorite person on this planet, in any version of reality. You're my best friend, my mother, my reason to go further than I ever thought possible.

Thank you so much for making this possibility one that I know I can navigate.

Thank you for giving me so many possibilities.

ABOUT THE AUTHOR

A.G.LEDESMA

A.G.Ledesma was born in Garden City, Kansas and attended Wichita State University. She has resided in Newton, Kansas since 2011. POSSIBILITY is Ledesma's literary debut as a poet.

You can connect with Ledesma through her social media.

IG: a.g.ledesma

TWT: aliahgledesma

agledesma.pub@gmail.com for inquiries

www.ingramcontent.com/pod-product-compliance
Lightning Source LLC
Chambersburg PA
CBHW030830090426
42737CB00009B/949